A
LESSON
FROM
ALOES

A LESSON FROM ALOES

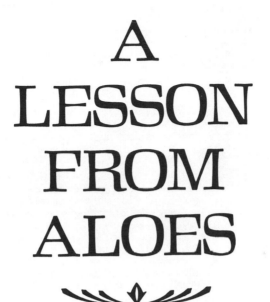

A Play by
Athol Fugard

Theatre Communications Group
New York

TCG gratefully acknowledges public funds from the National Endowment for
the Arts, the New York State Council on the Arts and the New York City
Department of Cultural Affairs, in addition to the generous support of the
following foundations and corporations: Alcoa Foundation; Ameritech Founda-
tion; ARCO Foundation; AT&T Foundation; Beatrice Foundation; Center for
Arts Criticism; Citicorp/Citibank; Common Wealth Fund; Consolidated Edison
Company of New York; Eleanor Naylor Dana Charitable Trust; Dayton Hudson
Foundation; Exxon Corporation; Ford Foundation; Japan–United States Friend-
ship Commission; Jerome Foundation; Andrew W. Mellon Foundation; Mobil
Foundation; National Broadcasting Company; New York Community Trust;
New York Times Company Foundation; Pew Charitable Trusts; Philip Morris
Companies; Rockefeller Foundation; Scherman Foundation; Shell Oil Company
Foundation; Shubert Foundation; Lila Wallace–Reader's Digest Fund; Xerox
Foundation.

A Lesson from Aloes was originally published in the United States
by Random House, Inc.

Frontis: Harris Yulin and James Earl Jones in the 1980 Yale Repertory
Theatre production, directed by Athol Fugard.
On the Cover: James Earl Jones, Maria Tucci and Harris Yulin. All
photographs © 1981 by Gerry Goodstein.

Library of Congress Cataloging in Publication Data
Fugard, Athol.
A Lesson from Aloes.
I. Title.
PR9369.3.F8L4 1981   822   80-6040
ISBN 1-55936-001-1   AACR2

First TCG edition: September 1989

In celebration of
Elizabeth Magdalena Potgieter

The first entry in my notebooks dealing with the people and events that would provide me with my main ideas and images for *A Lesson from Aloes* dates back to 1961. In February of that year I noted the following:

Party at Betty M.'s last night. Tolly, bespectacled and quiet-spoken leftist, communicating a mood of tired defeat. In his fifties. "I tell you, this I believe now. What they want, they must take.for themselves. Just take it and forget about the whites or waiting for them to change."

Opposed in this opinion by Piet V. . . . red-faced, big-hearted Afrikaner. "We must stand together man. Together! Together we can take on the whole world. They need us, Tolly, and we need them. Hell man, when I take my bus out Cadles way at five in the afternoon, I see them. I see them with their backs straight and proud walking home." He was referring to the boycott of the local bus service by nonwhites. "It's the people, Tolly! And they shall inherit the earth!"

Piet's passion is English poetry. He quotes endlessly, relevantly and with feeling, the words sonorous and precise in his Afrikaans mouth. Byron, Shakespeare, Keats, Shelley, Dylan Thomas.

"We come to bury Tolly
Not to praise him."

Piet was born on a farm in the Alexandria district. "My people were God-fearing. We kneeled at night and our workers kneeled with us and prayed. There was no difference, man. I was brought up to respect and believe in the Christian principles. My friends were the little black children on the farm. Race relations didn't exist for us."

He tells the story of Soya, an African friend of his childhood, who returned to the district in the last stages of T.B. and died in the Settlers Hospital, Grahamstown. Both still young men. The hospital authorities phoned him and told him to collect the body.

"I wanted to bury him in a Christian manner. 'Lord let not this dust . . .' But they were hard times, Tolly. There was a drought in the district. I was building a dairy. I tore down the roof to get wood for the coffin. When we buried him, his people said to me: 'Inkosi, speak!' I looked down at the coffin. All I could say was 'There lies a good man.' . . . and then I walked away into the veld and had a bloody good cry."

Piet is now a bus driver. He stood as a Coloured representative in the constituency that was at that time claimed to be the largest in the world . . . from Bredasdorp in the Cape to Harding in Natal, and Calvinia in the North Western Cape. Incident that hurt him most was when he addressed a meeting in Korsten . . . a Coloured area . . . "Brothers and Sisters," and they laughed at him. "Hell man, that hurt."

Dennis B. his friend, Coloured schoolteacher, followed him around during the election campaign, organizing opposition to Piet. Dennis's feeling was that if a Coloured could not represent Coloureds, they would rather have no rep. at all.

A Govt. stooge they both despised eventually got in. Dennis thought that Piet, in coming so close to the truth and than compromising it, was more dangerous than the Govt. stooge who was obviously a fraud.

In the course of that year the following entries were also made.

May

Piet and his wife Gladys. Their simple little house in Algoa Park. She is English speaking and well educated by comparison with his few years at a farm school. Writes poetry, nothing published. When their house was searched recently by the Special Branch, they found her poems and read them all. This had a traumatic effect on her (rape?), and led to a nervous breakdown. Mentally disturbed for a number of years. Several visits to Fort England mental home in Grahamstown. The last time she had to be taken forcibly after P.'s cajoling, pleading and threats had failed to get her voluntarily into the ambulance.

By contrast, P.'s sober sanity. The feeling he gives that this is indestructible . . . that you could destroy him but never drive him mad. She is highly strung, neurotic at her best, really unbalanced at her worse . . . the refinements and sensitivities that go with this condition. A qualified shorthand typist but has seldom kept a job for longer than a month because of the recurrent delusion that any new appointment in the office where she is working is a Special Branch spy placed to keep an eye on her and Piet.

September

The ship carrying Steve Tobias away from South Africa on an Exit Permit (the one-way ticket into voluntary exile) was passing out at sea when I walked the dogs at nine tonight. A day of bad weather . . . sudden squalls of wind and rain off the sea . . . the authentic S'kop spring, tolerable because of the promise that tomorrow will be a good day. Even so, Lisa and I found a break in the weather for a marvelous walk with the dogs.

And so, Steve. His last story, two days ago in Korsten, of interrogation by the Special Branch. He is convinced they tried to drive him to suicide. After one spell of questioning they pushed him into a room and into a chair beside an open window . . . six stories up. The policeman with him sat at least fifteen feet away . . . smiling all the time. Every five minutes or so the door opened and a captain just stood there, laughing mockingly and gloatingly at him. For Steve a moment of total despair. He did actually contemplate suicide. My last meeting with him in his little house at Schauder Township. A number of elderly Coloured women were there, making us coffee and digging up the plants in the garden.

Steve: The little guaya tree?

Aunt Betty: No, he's out. Down at Johnny's place. I planted it there this afternoon.

The African man, Lucas, who came around to say goodbye and offered a ten-rand note. "Buy fruit for the children. They say it's expensive in England."

November

An image which defines Piet and a human predicament. Thinking back to the drought, he cries out, "I'm frightened of being useless!" The logos behind his humanity, his politics. He escaped the horror of his impotence on the parched, dying land, by a life of action among men. And then the second "drought" (suspected by all that he is an informer), and again alone, just himself, empty-handed and useless. Piet face-to-face with himself . . . the absurdity of himself, *alone.*

"A man's scenery is other men."

During the next ten years I made several attempts to tell the story of Piet, Gladys and Steve. When the last of these miscarried in 1971 I thought I had finally abandoned the idea. Then, two years ago, and without any apparent external provocation, my memories of Piet, Gladys and Steve returned to me very obsessively and I started working on the play once again. A year later I went into rehearsals in Johannesburg with *A Lesson from Aloes.*

In thinking about the protracted history of this play as compared with the others I have written, I am conscious of one thing: the completion of a work has always depended on a correspondence, a relevance, between the external specifics of the play—the "story" as such—and my sense of myself at the time. In the case of *A Lesson from Aloes* this correspondence occurred significantly for the first time two years ago. Most of the reasons why this was the case are private, but there is one that I am prepared to try to articulate. Aloes are distinguished above all else for their inordinate capacity for survival in the harshest of possible environments. In writing this play I have at one level tried to examine and question the possibility and nature of survival in a country for which "drought," with its harsh and relentless resonances, is a very apt metaphor.

Athol Fugard
New Haven
2/2/80

Characters

PIET BEZUIDENHOUT   An Afrikaner, in his
                          mid-forties.
GLADYS BEZUIDENHOUT   His wife, the same age.
STEVE DANIELS   His friend, a Coloured
                          man, the same age.

The action of the play moves between two areas representing the backyard and the bedroom of a small house in Algoa Park, Port Elizabeth.

Act One

The backyard. It is cluttered with a collection of aloes in a variety of tins of all shapes and sizes.
There is a gate with a nameboard: Xanadu.
PIET, *seated at a garden table with an aloe in front of him, is studying a small field book on the plants. He is wearing spectacles, short trousers, no shirt and sandals without socks.* GLADYS, *behind sunglasses, sits very still on a garden bench.*
Time: late afternoon.

PIET *(Reading from the book)* ". . . small, glaucous leaves, erect or incurved . . ."*(Studies the specimen in front of him, then turns back to the book)* "Tuberculate-based . . ."*(Turns to the glossary at the back of the book)* Tuberculate . . . "Having knobby or warty excrescences."*(Back to the entry he was reading)* "Tuberculate-based soft prickles on both surfaces." *(He holds the book at arm's length for a comparison between the illustration and his plant. He shakes his head)* No. That's not it.
    (He closes the book, and takes off the spectacles. He gets up quietly, the aloe in his hands, and looks at GLADYS*)*

GLADYS *(Without moving)* I'm awake.

3

PIET   Well, my dear, we have a stranger in our midst. Aloe Anonymous! Because that is what it is until I know its name. I've been through my book twice, page by page, but there is nothing that looks quite like it. I don't think I can allow myself to believe I've discovered a new species. That would be something! I'd name it after you, my dear. Hail aloe Gladysiensis! Sounds rather good, doesn't it? *(He reads the other aloes)*   Hail ferox! And you aristata . . . arborescens . . . ciliaris . . . and now Gladysiensis! Welcome to the most noble order of Eastern Cape aloes. An impressive array of names, isn't it? And knowing them is important. It makes me feel that little bit more at home in my world. And yet, as little Juliet once said: "What's in a name? That which we call a rose/By any other name would smell as sweet." *(These lines, and all his other quotations, although delivered with a heavy Afrikaans accent, are said with a sincere appreciation of the words involved. He thinks about those he has just quoted)*   Alas, it's not as simple as that, is it?

GLADYS   Are you talking to me?

PIET   Who else, my dear?

GLADYS   The aloes . . . or yourself. I'm never sure these days.

PIET   Names are more than just labels. *(He sits beside her on the bench)*   Petrus Jacobus Bezuidenhout. *(He gives a little smile)*   "So, would Petrus, were he not Petrus called,/Retain that dear perfection which he owns without that title?"

GLADYS   What are you talking about?

4

PIET   The balcony scene. Where the little lady laments Romeo's name. I was just thinking about mine, trying to hear it as others do.

GLADYS   And?

PIET   Nothing . . . except that when other men say Piet Bezuidenhout it is me they are talking about. Yes! That is what's in a name. My face, my story in mine, as much as theirs, is in *Romeo and Juliet.* "Then deny thy father and refuse thy name." Hell! I don't know about those Italians, but that's a hard one for an Afrikaner. No. For better or for worse, I will remain positively identified as Petrus Jacobus Bezuidenhout; Species, Afrikaner; Habitat, Algoa Park, Port Elizabeth, in this year of our Lord, 1963 . . . and accept the consequences.
   (He looks at his wrist watch)

GLADYS   What is the time now?

PIET   Just on four o'clock.

GLADYS   It's passing very slowly, isn't it?

PIET   Yes, it is. The sun is as lazy as we are this afternoon.

GLADYS   *(Shaking her head)*   It's because we're waiting.

PIET   Let me get you something to read.

GLADYS   I'm all right.

PIET   I've got today's paper inside.

GLADYS   Stop fussing, Peter. I've learned how to sit and wait. When should we expect them?

5

PIET I didn't fix a definite time. I just said, "Supper." So what do you think? Half-past six? Seven? They won't be too late because of the children. If we start to get ready at five, we should be all right. Everything under control in the kitchen?

GLADYS Yes.

PIET Then relax, my dear. Enjoy the sunshine.

GLADYS I'm perfectly relaxed.

PIET Good.

GLADYS You're the one who can't keep still.

PIET (*He moves back to the garden table where we first saw him*) Just tidying up my mess.

GLADYS I hope I'm not getting too much sun.

PIET No danger of that on an autumn afternoon. This is the start of our gentle time, Gladys . . . our season of mists and mellow fruitfulness, close bosom friend of the maturing sun. On the farm there was almost a sense of the veld sighing with relief when autumn finally set in. We certainly did. Man and animal. Months of grace while we waited for the first rains.

GLADYS My skin can't take it. I learned that lesson when I was a little girl.

PIET Sunburn.

GLADYS Yes. A holiday somewhere with my mother and father. On the very first day I picked up too much sun on the beach and that was the end of it.

6

My mother dabbed me all over with calamine lotion to soothe the pain. I can remember looking at myself in the mirror . . . a frightened little white ghost. Mommy was terrified that I was going to end up with a brown skin. But she needn't have worried. It all peeled away and there I was, the same as before.

PIET   The voortrekker women had the same problem. That's where the old white bonnet comes from. Protection.

GLADYS   I think it was Cape Town. Not that it made any difference where I was. All I remember of the outside world was standing at a window and watching the dogs in the street go beserk when the dirt-boys came to empty the bins. Heavens! What a terrible commotion that was. A big gray lorry with its mountain of rubbish, the black men banging on its side shouting, the dogs going for them savagely . . . *(Breaking out of her reverie)*   I think I need my sun hat.

PIET   Don't move. *(He walks to the back door)*   Where is it?

GLADYS   In the bedroom.
      (PIET goes into the house—the bedroom—and returns a few seconds later with the sun hat)

PIET   Here you are, my dear. *(Gladys doesn't take the sun hat)*   Anything wrong?

GLADYS   Did I put away my diary?

PIET   I didn't notice.

(After a moment's hesitation, GLADYS *walks awkwardly into the house)*

GLADYS I'll . . . I'll just . . . *(She enters the bedroom and unlocks a dressing-table drawer and takes out her personal diary. She looks around the room and then hides it under the mattress on the bed. She steadies herself and returns to* PIET*)* Safe and sound.

PIET I'll never interfere with it, my dear.

GLADYS I know that!

PIET So, where were we? Yes, our nameless friend. *(He holds up the unidentified aloe)* I'll have to wait for it to flower. That makes identification much easier. And it will! It's got no choice. I've put it in a tin, so it needs me now. A little neglect on my side and it will be into a drought as fearsome as anything out there in the veld. If plants have feelings, this is as bad as keeping animals in cages. It's the roots that upset me. Even with all my care and attention they are still going to crawl around inside this little tin and tie themselves into knots looking for the space creation intended for them.

GLADYS *(Obviously not listening to him)* And you are quite certain they're bringing the children?

PIET Yes. I very definitely made it an invitation to the whole family. It's high time we saw our godson again. Children grow fast at his age. And little Lucille should be quite the young lady by now.

GLADYS How many of them are there again?

PIET Steve and Mavis, the three girls, little Pietertjie and then the two of us. Eight all told. It will be quite a party. Have we got enough to feed the hungry hordes?

GLADYS *(Betraying her nervousness)* More than enough. That's not going to be the problem.

PIET Then what is? *(GLADYS doesn't answer)* They're not strangers, Gladys. It's Steve and his family.

GLADYS It's a big family.

PIET We've had them all here before and you coped splendidly.

GLADYS That was some time ago. I'm out of practice, remember. I know what's going to happen. You and Steven will end up in a corner talking politics all night and I'll be left with the rest of them, trying to make polite conversation. I can't even remember their names, Peter!

PIET Mavis, Lucille, Charmaine . . .

GLADYS And then that little boy . . . !

PIET Yes, I know. Little Pietertjie can get a bit boisterous at times, but don't worry, my dear. Steven knows how to handle him. You must admit the girls are well behaved. You always admired their manners, remember? Please and thank you and speak when you're spoken to. Please relax, my dear. You won't have any trouble.

GLADYS Well . . . you can't deny we are going to be crowded.

PIET   Yes, I do. Observe. *(Placing two tables in front of the garden bench)* The festive board! *(Positioning chairs. He works hard at trying to allay* GLADYS's *anxieties)* The Lord and Lady of the Manor . . . our two honored guests . . . and then in descending order of age . . . Lucille, Charmaine, Beryl and little Pietertjie. (*GLADYS studies the seating arrangement in silence)* Does that look crowded?

GLADYS   No.

PIET   Then what's the matter?

GLADYS   You've got the little boy next to me.

PIET   Because Steve is sitting there and I thought . . . All right, all right! We'll change it around. In ascending order of age: Pietertjie here and then Beryl, Charmaine and Lucille next to you. How's that?

GLADYS   Thank you. It's not that I don't like children . . .

PIET   Say no more, my dear. I understand. *(He surveys the table)* We mustn't forget your brass candlesticks. That was an inspired thought. Alfresco and candlelight. It's going to look very good. Continental!

GLADYS   Don't expect too much from me. I can only manage cold meats and salads.

PIET   Have we got a little pudding?

GLADYS   Yes. Jelly and custard. I've tried my best, Peter!

PIET   I know that, my dear. I was just thinking of the children.

GLADYS   If you want the menu, it's assorted cold meats . . . ham, brawn and polony . . . three salads . . . potato mayonnaise . . .

PIET   What could be better? A cold buffet! It's going to be a warm evening. I must remember to chill the wine.
(Looks at his wrist watch)

GLADYS   *(Anxiously)*   Is it time?

PIET   No, not yet.

GLADYS   How much longer?

PIET   Let's try to forget it, my dear, and enjoy what's left of the afternoon. That's why it's passing slowly. We're flattering time with too much attention.

GLADYS   You can't exactly blame us. They'll be our first visitors since I've been back. *(She waits for* PIET *to respond. He doesn't)*   You do realize that, don't you?

PIET   Yes, now that you mention it. All the more reason for a celebration.

GLADYS   I won't have any trouble finding something to write in my diary tonight. "At last! Other people! Just when it was beginning to feel as if Peter and I were the last two left in the world. Steven and his family came to supper."

PIET   *(Back with his unidentified aloe)*   So . . . What I'll do is make some notes and go to the library and sit down with Gilbert Westacott Reynolds—*The Aloes of South Africa.* A formidable prospect! Five hundred and sixteen big pages of small print . . . and that is not counting General Smuts's foreword. A lifetime's work so that ignoramuses like myself can point to an aloe and say its name. And make no mistake about it . . . I want to. So . . . let us attempt a sketch. What is it that makes knowing them so important?

GLADYS Aloes?

PIET No, their names. Just names in general. Yours, mine . . . anything! There's a lot of mystery in them, isn't there?

GLADYS Peter and Gladys Bezuidenhout, Xanadu, 27 Kraaibos Street, Algoa Park. It sounds very ordinary to me.

PIET Because it's your own. Familiarity has bred contempt. I can remember very clearly how, when we first met, "Gladys Adams" was a name to conjure with.

GLADYS Oh come, Peter!

PIET It's the truth, my dear. How did you feel about mine?

GLADYS I liked it. Very much. It was certainly much longer than anything I'd hoped for. I thought it had a strong earthy sound . . .

PIET Yes, it has that. Bezuidenhout! Origin: Dutch. The first one arrived in 1695.

GLADYS But to be quite frank, I wasn't sure that Gladys went with it.

PIET Really? Gladys Bezuidenhout. Sounds all right to me.

GLADYS Familiarity has bred contempt, Peter.

PIET Touché! But it goes even deeper than that. What's the first thing we give a child when it's born? A name. Or when strangers meet, what is the first thing they do? Exchange names. According to the Bible, that was the very first thing Adam did in Eden. He named his world. "And whatsoever Adam called every living creature, that was the name thereof." No. There is no rest for me until I've identified this.

GLADYS Can I see it?
    (He passes her the aloe)

PIET *(Looking in his field book)* This is the nearest I could get to it. Aloe humilis. But it's not right, is it?

GLADYS They all look alike to me. Thorns and fat, fleshy leaves.

PIET Of course. The distinguishing characteristics of the genus, the family being *Liliaceae*. Protection against grazing animals and the storage of moisture during periods of drought. But what species?! Ay, there's the rub.

GLADYS Do any of them have any scent?

PIET   No. That they don't have. But the old people used to make a purgative from the bitter juice of the leaves. And they are mentioned in the Bible.

GLADYS   Really, Peter! That doesn't help them. Purgatives and the Bible! It only makes it worse.

PIET   How do you mean?

GLADYS   Well, they're not very pretty plants, you know. Is there a good word for something you can't and don't want to touch? That would describe them.

PIET   A rose has also got its thorns.

GLADYS   There's no comparison! They've got a lovely scent, they're pretty to look at and so many beautiful colors. But these . . . *(She pushes the aloe away)* No, thank you.

PIET   *(Looking around at his collection)*   This is not fair to them. An aloe isn't seen to its best advantage in a jam tin in a little backyard. They need space. The open veld with purple mountains in the distance. This one . . . arborescens . . . I think it is possibly my favorite . . . we had one on the farm growing around a goat kraal. Eight-, ten-foot high and so thick a chicken couldn't push its way through. You should have seen that when it was flowering. A veritable forest of scarlet spikes with the little suikerbekkies . . . honey birds . . . sucking up the nectar. Or even old ferox, with all its thorns! A hillside covered with them in bloom! "Damp clods with corn may thank the showers/But when the desert boulder flowers/No common buds unfold." Roy

Campbell. He understood them. "A glory such as from scant seed/The thirsty rocks suffice, to breed/ Out of the rainless glare." And remember, it's a defiant glory, Gladys. That veld is a hard world. They and the thorn trees were just about the only things still alive in it when I finally packed up the old truck and left the farm. Four years of drought, but they were flowering once again. I'm ashamed to say it, but I resented them for that. It's a small soul that resents a flower, but I suppose mine was when I drove away and saw them there in the veld, surviving where I had failed.

GLADYS   Is that the price of survival in this country? Thorns and bitterness.

PIET   For the aloe it is. Maybe there's some sort of lesson for us there.

GLADYS   What do you mean?

PIET   We need survival mechanisms as well.

GLADYS   Speak for yourself, Peter. I'm a human being not a . . . prickly pear. (PIET *stares at her, appalled*) What's the matter?

PIET   The prickly pear isn't an aloe, Gladys.

GLADYS   Please, Peter . . . !

PIET   It's not even indigenous, my dear. The jointed cactus is a declared weed.

GLADYS   This conversation is upsetting me, Peter.

PIET   Sorry, my dear. What . . .

(GLADYS moves abruptly into the house. She returns a few seconds later with a tablecloth, which she tries, without too much success because of her agitation, to spread over the "festive board")

PIET   Sorry, my dear. What have I said?

GLADYS   We've already had droughts, prickly pears and despair. I suppose we'll be into politics next and the black man's misery. I'm not exaggerating, Peter. That is what a conversation with you has become— a catalogue of South African disasters. And you never stop! You seem to have a perverse need to dwell on what is cruel and ugly about this country. Is there nothing gentle in your world?

PIET   Is it really as bad as that?

GLADYS   Yes, it is. And don't make me feel guilty for saying it. *(She gestures at the aloes)*   Look at them! Is that what you hope for? To be like one of them? That's not the only possibility in life, you know. If that's what your expectations have shrunk to, it's your business, but God has not planted me in a jam tin. He might have cursed you Afrikaners, but not the whole human race. I want to live my life, not just survive it. I know I'm in this backyard with them, but that is not going to happen to me.

PIET   I . . . *(He makes a helpless gesture)*   . . . What can I say? I'm sorry you don't like them.

GLADYS   Don't like them! It's worse than that, Peter. *(He looks at her)*   I'm going to be very honest with you. They frighten me. Yes, thorns and bitterness?

I'm afraid there's more than that to them. They're turgid with violence, like everything else in this country. And they're trying to pass it on to me.

PIET *(Carefully)* What do you mean, my dear?

GLADYS Don't worry. I won't let it happen. I won't!
(She pauses)

PIET *(Trying to break the mood)* Well . . . *(Looks at his wrist watch)* Time to get ready. They'll be here soon.

GLADYS *(Looking fearful)* Who?

PIET Steve and Mavis.
(They pause, looking at each other)

GLADYS Yes, of course.

PIET I'll look after the table.

GLADYS *(Moving her hands to her face)* I think I have picked up too much sun, you know. I feel quite flushed. I wonder if we've got any calamine lotion in the house?
(She goes into the house. PIET adjusts the tablecloth and follows her)

The bedroom. GLADYS *is at her dressing table. There is a knock on the door. She tenses.*

PIET Can I come in? *(Pause)* Gladys!

GLADYS Yes?

PIET Can I come in?

GLADYS One moment. *(She looks back abruptly at her bed, where her diary is hidden. She retrieves it, and after a few desperate seconds of trying to find another hiding place, sits down with it at her dressing table)* All right!
    *(*PIET *enters. He has a towel around his waist, having just bathed)*

PIET I thought you might be changing.

GLADYS I will in a minute.

PIET Well, I'll make a start. I won't be long. *(In the course of this scene he changes into a safari suit, with short trousers, long socks and brown shoes)* Shorts won't be out of place, will they? It's not really a formal occasion, and it is outdoors. I am sure you ladies will look after the finery.
    (He becomes conscious of her sitting very still at the dressing table)

PIET Were you busy with your diary?

GLADYS What do you mean?

PIET Making your entry for the day.

GLADYS It's too early for that. Nothing has happened yet.

PIET True. But, as you said, my dear, you will certainly have subject matter tonight.

GLADYS I was just paging through it.

PIET Reading the old ones.

GLADYS That's right. Reminding myself of the exciting life I've been living. *(She opens her diary, but in such a way that he can't see it)* This hasn't been such a good week. Let's see . . . an old woman looking for work, the meter reader . . . who else? Oh yes! Those little black boys selling brooms and baskets. But they're always around. Last week I had a gentleman from the Watchtower Society at the front door. That was a long talk. I was a bit nervous at first because he asked if he could come in, but he turned out to be very nice. Do you know they've got a date worked out for the end of the world? It's not far off, either. I almost told him there are times when I think it has already happened. *(PIET smiles)* I'm not joking. It can be very quiet here in the house when you're at work. If I haven't got the radio on or a car isn't passing in the street, it's hard sometimes to believe there is a world out there full of other people. Just you and me. That's all that's left. The streets are empty and I imagine you wandering around looking for another survivor. If you ever find one, Peter, you must bring him home.

PIET   Well, I've got news for you. I found six of them and they'll be arriving in a short while. I know it's been a quiet time, but under the circumstances, don't you think that's been for the best?

GLADYS   *(With a little laugh)*   Quiet time! You're an unpredictable mixture of understatement and exaggeration. I never know which to expect. How long have I been back? Six months? Seven?

PIET   Nearly seven.

GLADYS   And you don't find it strange that in all that time not one of our friends has been around to see us, or invited us to see them? Solly, or Mervyn, or Betty . . . there was never any shortage of comrades in the old days. Is it because of me?

PIET   No. You mustn't think that.

GLADYS   Then say something! Every time I mention it you either ignore me, or change the subject.

PIET   *(Trying to placate her)*   All right, my dear! Relax.

GLADYS   God I wish you would stop saying that!

PIET   There's no mystery, Gladys. A lesson in human nature maybe, but that's all. It's a dangerous time and people are frightened.

GLADYS   Of what?

PIET   Isn't that obvious?

GLADYS   I don't know. You tell me.

PIET   The police raids, then Steve going to jail, the banning of the congress . . . everyone has crawled away into his own little shell. It's as simple as that. Why do you shake your head?

GLADYS   It's too simple.

PIET   Most explanations of human behavior usually are.
   (He makes a move to leave the bedroom)

GLADYS   Peter . . .

PIET   Yes, my dear?

GLADYS   Is there something I don't know?

PIET   *(Evenly)*   If there is, I know nothing about it as well.

GLADYS   Then I am even more surprised at how easily you accept the situation.

PIET   I don't accept it easily, but there is nothing else to do. I can't change human nature.

GLADYS   Not even a complaint about its lack of courage and faith. After all it has meant the end of "The Cause."

PIET   No. I don't want to sit in judgment on others.

GLADYS   And what about you, Peter?

PIET   Why should I be any different? Anyone is justified in feeling nervous and uneasy these days.

21

GLADYS   The word was frightened. *(She pauses)*   Well?

PIET   Yes, I am.

GLADYS   That's very hard to believe. Watching you with your aloes, quoting your poetry . . . in spite of all that has happened, you've still got a whole world intact. You seem very safe to me.

PIET   The aloes give me pleasure, Gladys, not a purpose. *(She smiles)*   What's the matter?

GLADYS   *(Closing her eyes)*   Don't say anything! I am going to try to remember. And no prompting. *(She quotes from memory)*   "There is a purpose to life, and we will be measured by the extent to which we harness ourselves to it." And the author . . . Thoreau.

PIET   Correct.

GLADYS   Word perfect?

PIET   Yes.

GLADYS   *(Delighted with herself)*   So I get full marks! That's encouraging. After all, it was quite a few years ago. Can you remember when?

PIET   No.

GLADYS   Oh, Peter! How sad. Our very first meeting . . . the concert . . . when you walked me home afterward.

PIET   Yes, yes, of course. I had forgotten.

GLADYS But I'm cheating a little. I only remember it that clearly because I wrote it down that night and read it to myself many times afterward. That's how my diaries started, you know. The very first entry. I was so impressed with the words and your faith in them. *(Closing her eyes again as she tries to remember)* You said good night to me on the verandah and I let myself into the house. My mother was still awake, and angry. I tried to apologize to her for being late, but she wouldn't accept it. Just sat there in bed, propped up against her pillows, ignoring me. I made her a cup of Ovaltine, went to my room, sat down at the dressing table and wrote: "There is a purpose to life..." *(Very proud of herself)* How's that?

PIET Very good.

GLADYS Do you still believe it?

PIET Yes. It's not as easy as it used to be, but I still do.

GLADYS I envy you, as I did then. Nothing seemed more without purpose than the Gladys Adams I looked at in the mirror, in that stale room, with my mother sick and sulking on the other side of the wall. She had a purpose. A terrible determination not to die. I'm not exaggerating. Dr. Finnemore said her last six years were a miracle. I was convinced she was going to live longer than me. At times I still find it hard to believe that she is dead and I'm the one who's alive. It's very unfair. That was another entry in the first diary. "My mother died today. I haven't cried yet, and I don't think I'm going to."

PIET   Don't brood about bygones, my dear. It's all over and done with. *(Trying to change the subject)* That one must be nearly full now.

GLADYS   How do you know?

PIET   Page a day. It's nearly a year since I gave it to you.

GLADYS   *(Sharply)*   I see. It's going to be like a birthday, is it, or our anniversary. A date that mustn't be forgotten. "Give Gladys another diary."

PIET   Right. I'll forget it if you want me to.

GLADYS   Just like that? That's more than I could do.

PIET   I'll try.

GLADYS   No, don't do that. It was a very touching gesture, even though I wasn't in a state to appreciate it at the time. *(Opening the diary)* I've kept the card. I use it as a marker. *(Reading)* "Take this sweet soul! We'll start again./They've come and gone and all in vain/For we live on." It was so appropriate. Where does it come from?

PIET   Henry Wadsworth Longfellow.

GLADYS   *(Holding her diary)*   I'd be lost without this. It's where I keep all my little secrets. A woman needs them, and as you know, I did lose all of those I once had. You were given a receipt for them, remember? A little piece of paper torn from a grubby notebook.

PIET   Yes, I do. But that is something we must try to forget, Gladys, not remember.

GLADYS Yes, I realize that. But I can't help myself sometimes. There's so much that keeps reminding me. After all, it was in this very room. He sat
down here, opened the first one, and started to
read . . .

PIET *(His desperation growing)* I remember it very
clearly, my love! I was here! With you! *(He pauses)*
Maybe if we changed the room around . . . rear-
ranged the furniture! That might help. What do you
think?

GLADYS You could try.

PIET I know what it really needs, though. More light!
This is a dark little room. I know what that means.
I've had my occasions to sit brooding in them as
well. That's the answer, Gladys! As soon as we've
got a little something together in the bank again I'm
going to put another window in that wall. Light!
That's what we need. And we'll change the furniture as well. It will be a different room. I should
have thought of it before.

GLADYS *(She hasn't been listening to him)* Yes . . . you
led them in and then stood there next to the door-
way. I can't remember much about you after that.
I was still trying to get into my dressing gown.
Then the one in charge saw them on the table, asked
you what they were . . . you told him . . . he apolo-
gized to me nicely and started to read them . . . page
by page. I couldn't believe it was happening. Did I
ever get my dressing gown on?

PIET Please . . .

GLADYS *(Violently)* That's an important question, Peter! Did I ever get my dressing gown on?

PIET No.

GLADYS So I just stood there . . . ! What did I look like?

PIET For God's sake, Gladys! What do you want?

GLADYS An answer to a simple question! What did I look like?

PIET You had just woken up, you were sleepy, you didn't know what was going on . . .

GLADYS *(She gazes into the dressing-table mirror)* Me. *(Pause)*

PIET They won't visit us again, Gladys.

GLADYS What makes you so sure of that?

PIET Because there is nothing to be found here, and they know it. They're not fools. *Please* believe me. Where's my Bible?
(He finds it on a bedside table)

GLADYS What are you going to do with that?

PIET Listen to me now. On this book . . . on my mother's grave . . .

GLADYS Oh shut up! Just say what you want to.

PIET The search that night had nothing to do with you personally. They were looking for . . . God knows what! . . . banned literature, political secrets that didn't exist.

GLADYS   And instead they found my diaries, and they did take them away and they haven't given them back!

PIET   I'm still trying. That's why I've kept the receipt.

GLADYS   *(Outraged)*   You what?

PIET   Kept the receipt.

GLADYS   Get it. *(He hesitates)*   Where's that receipt, Peter? *(He produces it from inside the Bible.   She can barely articulate)*   What's written on it?

PIET   *(Reading the scrap of paper)*   "Gladys Bezuidenhout's diaries . . ." then Strydom's signature, the date and our address.

GLADYS   Tear it up. *(He hesitates)*   Tear it up! Small pieces. *(He does so.   She holds out her hand, takes the pieces and puts them down carefully on the dressing table. For a few seconds she lapses into an almost bland normality)*   There. I've cancelled those years. I'm going to forget I ever lived them. They weren't just laundry lists, you know. There were very intimate and personal things in those diaries, things a woman only talks about to herself. Even then it took me a lot of trust and courage to do that. I know I never had much of either, but I was learning. *(Her hysteria begins to surface again)*   You were such a persuasive teacher, Peter! "Trust, Gladys. Trust yourself. Trust life." There's nothing left of that. *(She brandishes her diary)*   Must I tell you what I've been trying to do with this all day? Hide it. It's been behind the dressing table . . . under the mattress

27

. . . Can you think of somewhere really safe? Where nobody would find it, including yourself? There isn't, is there? Do you know what I would really like to do with this? Make you eat it and turn it into shit . . . then maybe everybody would leave it alone. Yes, you heard me correctly. Shit! I've learned how to use my dirty words. And just as well, because there's no other adequate vocabulary for this country. Maybe I should do that in case they come again. A page full of filthy language. Because that is what they were really hoping for when they sat down with my diaries. Filth!

PIET   I don't know what to say.

GLADYS   Thank God! Because if you were to tell me once more that they won't come again . . . ! To start with, I don't believe you, but even if I did, that once was enough. You seem to have a lot of difficulty understanding that, Peter. It only needs to happen to a woman once, for her to lose all trust she ever had in anything or anybody. They violated me, Peter. I might just as well have stayed in that bed, lifted up my nightdress and given them each a turn. I've shocked you. Good! Then maybe now you understand. Yes, I can see it. You are frightened.

PIET   That's right.

GLADYS   Of me?

PIET   For you. Please be careful.

GLADYS   You're too late with that advice. You should have given it to the Gladys Adams you conjured with, instead of persuading her that life was to be trusted. Not that she needed it. She'd been warned. She knew the dogs are mad.

PIET   What do you mean?

GLADYS   Exactly what I've said. Our dogs are mad. They're guarding our dirtbins, not us. I discovered that as a little girl. Forgetting it was the biggest mistake I ever made . . . and it was you who made me do it. Are you feeling guilty?

PIET   Yes. I know that nothing of what you've been through would have happened if you hadn't married me.

GLADYS   That's perfectly true. Which makes you as responsible for my condition as them. *(Stopping herself)*   No . . . No . . . ! Why don't you stop me?

PIET   *(Nearly frantic)*   I can't! I've tried.

GLADYS   *(Appalled)*   I didn't mean that. I'm sorry. *(She pauses . . . then quietly . . .)*   What are we going to do, Peter?

PIET   About tonight?

GLADYS   And tomorrow . . . and the next day . . .

PIET   *(Trying his utmost to calm her down)*   I know. First thing . . . I want you to lie down and relax in a nice hot bath. I'll run it for you. Just lie down and relax. And while you're doing that, I'll take a bus into Gelvandale and put off Steve and Mavis . . .

GLADYS   No.

PIET   Just listen! I'll take the wine I bought and have a drink with them at their place. It won't be obvious. I'll say . . . something has come up at work . . . overtime . . .

GLADYS   No. Don't you think we're coping with enough lies already? Let them come. I'll be all right. *(PIET is not convinced. GLADYS puts her diary down on the dressing table)* There. No more hiding it away . . . or anything. Don't you trust me?

PIET   Of course I do. But are you quite sure you want them to come?

GLADYS   Yes. And to prove it, I'd like to change now, please.

PIET   Sorry, my dear. I'll . . . I'll start to get things ready.

GLADYS   *(As he is leaving the room)* I am trying, Peter.

PIET   I know that. *(PIET goes out, leaving GLADYS alone at the dressing table)*

The backyard. PIET *is laying the table.* GLADYS *comes out of the house. She has changed and has a shawl over her shoulders. Her manner—quiet and composed—is in direct contrast to the violence and hysteria in the bedroom.* PIET *watches her expectantly. She goes to the table.*

GLADYS   Is this where Mavis sits?

PIET   Yes. (GLADYS *places a little parcel on the table)* What is it, my dear?

GLADYS   A small gesture, that's all. A little embroidered handkerchief. It's not very much, but the needlework is very fine. My mother would never let a visitor leave the house without some little souvenir of the occasion.

PIET   That's a lovely thought, Gladys. And you look splendid!

GLADYS   Thank you. *(She looks at the table)* Well, you're quite right, Peter. It is going to look very good.

PIET   Everyman's altar to the civilized virtues . . . a well-laid table with food waiting and friends coming. The candlesticks create a sense of occasion, don't they? You wouldn't like to do your fancy thing with the serviettes, would you?

GLADYS   If it will make you happy. *(She sits down at the table and starts to fold them)* You look nervous, Peter. Please don't worry about me. I promise everything will be all right.

PIET   I can see that! I'm just overanxious for us all to have a good time tonight.
       (He takes a little book out of his pocket)

GLADYS   What are you reading?

PIET   My little book of quotations. I'm looking for a few strong lines for a toast when we sit down to eat.

GLADYS   What have you found?

PIET   *(Opening the book and reading)* Where is it? . . . Where is it? . . . Yes! "Sweet is the scene where genial friendship plays/The pleasing game of interchanging praise." Oliver Wendell Holmes. There's that. Then this: "What is the odds so long as the fire of soul is kindled at the taper of conviviality, and the wing of friendship never moults a feather." Charles Dickens. Or this: "Thy friendship oft has made my heart to ache:/Do be my enemy—for friendship's sake." William Blake.

GLADYS   Let me hear the second one again.

PIET   "What is the odds so long as the fire of soul is kindled at the taper of conviviality . . ."

GLADYS   Yes, that's the one. Tapers . . . candles! It fits in.

PIET I never thought of that! Settled. I shall now commit it to memory.

(GLADYS *watches him as he paces up and down, memorizing the lines*)

GLADYS Steven means a lot to you, doesn't he?

PIET Yes, he does. After you, I owe him more than anybody else in this world. If it wasn't for Steve, I suppose I'd still be sitting in a little room somewhere hating rain . . . because it had come too late. That's how I ended up when I left the farm. A little room in Havelock Street. I used to pull the curtains and put cotton wool in my ears so that I wouldn't hear it.

GLADYS That doesn't sound like you.

PIET It was me all right. (*He goes into the house and returns with a few more items for the table*) Doesn't seem right, does it, that something so important in your life should depend on chance? Because that is all it was. It could just as easily not have happened. But one of the other bus drivers was sick one morning and they took me off the Humewood run and put me onto No. 11 . . . Market Square to Cadles. I was even fed up about it. Instead of that nice drive next to the sea, it was into that ugly Coloured area with all the factories. But it also happened to be the morning the bus boycott started. I'd heard talk about it in the sheds, but so what! It had nothing to do with me. Politics! . . . (*He smiles*) until I drove my empty bus through that crowd walking to work. Hell, Gladys, it was a sight! Men, women, even

school children, walking and laughing and full of
defiance. Bitter and hard as I was inside, I felt emo-
tions. At first I tried to ignore them. I said to myself
the people were being stupid. Why make an issue of
a penny? That's all the fares had been increased by.
But they didn't think that. They carried on walking
and waving at me and my empty bus. Steve had a
position on the corner of Standford and Kempston
roads. I'd see this man standing there handing out
pamphlets or addressing a little crowd. Then one
morning the police moved in and arrested him. I
was parked at a bus stop across the road when it
happened. Into the van he went and I thought that
was the end of it. Not a damn. Next day he was back
again. The comrades had bailed him out. That's
when I thought: To hell with it. I want to hear what
this little bugger is saying. And anyway my bus was
empty as usual. So I stopped and got out. I got a
little nervous with all of them watching me as I
walked over. I was the only white there. When I got
to them I said I just wanted to listen. The next thing
I knew is they were cheering and laughing and slap-
ping me on the back and making a place for me in
the front row. *(He pauses)* I don't know how to
describe it, Gladys . . . the effect that had on me. It
was like rain after a long drought. Being welcomed
by those people was the most moving thing that has
ever happened to me. Feelings about life and people,
which I thought had withered away like everything
else on the farm, were alive again. I was so emo-
tional I didn't even hear what Steve said when he
carried on talking. Something about a penny and
the price of bread. I fell in beside him when they
started walking and when he turned off to go to the

building site, where he was working, I carried on alone. Into town and straight to the head office where I handed in my notice. They docked off a week when they paid me out. Deserting my bus while on duty. The next day I was back on that same corner, and a week later I was handing out pamphlets with Steve. The bus company won in the end. They got that penny from the people. I thought we had failed, but not Steve. He said he'd expected it. The really important thing was that those two weeks of boycott had raised the political consciousness of the people. They had acted politically, some of them maybe for the first time in their lives. My first lesson from Steve, and the most important one. An evil system isn't a natural disaster. There's nothing you can do to stop a drought, but bad laws and social injustice are man-made and can be unmade by men. It's as simple as that. We can make this a better world to live in. (GLADYS *has been listening and watching very attentively*)   You've been very patient with me.

GLADYS   It wasn't difficult. I saw the man I first met very clearly again. It's been a hard time for you, hasn't it?

PIET   No more so than for everybody else, and certainly less than for Steve.

GLADYS   Well at least the two of you will be able to salvage your friendship tonight. (*A pause.* PIET *doesn't respond*)   That's at least some consolation, isn't it? (PIET *hesitates*)   What's the matter?

PIET   He's leaving, Gladys.

GLADYS What do you mean?

PIET Steve and Mavis and the children are leaving the country. They're going to settle in England.

GLADYS How do you know?

PIET He told me.

GLADYS For good?

PIET Yes.

GLADYS When?

PIET Next week. *(They pause, then* PIET *goes into the house and returns with something else for the table)*

GLADYS You're joking.

PIET I'm not.

GLADYS Well . . . that's a surprise . . . to say the least. Steven leaving. I always thought of him as being like you, hanging on to the bitter end. *(Shaking her head in disbelief)* I don't know what to say.

PIET Neither do I.

GLADYS *(Her tone hardening)* No. I'm wrong. I do. Good for Steven! And England! From all I've heard, it's a very different world to this one. They are very lucky.

PIET He's leaving on an exit permit, Gladys.

GLADYS So?

PIET He can't come back.

GLADYS So!

PIET I don't think it's all that easy for him. This is his home as much as it is ours.

GLADYS No. I know I was born here, but I will never call it that. Why didn't you tell me earlier?

PIET I don't know. Maybe because I also find it so hard to believe.

GLADYS Believe what? That he doesn't love "home" as much as you? It's almost a joke, you know, coming after all you've just been telling me.

PIET You're being very hard on him, my dear.

GLADYS Of course. Because I'm jealous. I'd never persuade you to go, would I?

PIET I haven't had to survive a banning order for three years and then six months in jail.

GLADYS That's not such a high price to pay for coming to your senses. I still think he's lucky and I still envy him for getting out.

PIET Anyway, he's certainly doing that. At first I thought he meant Middelburg or Graaff Reinet, or something like that. He's got family up there. That's where Mavis and the children went when he was inside. I think I said as much. But he just stood there on the pavement smiling at me in a funny sort of way. *(Shaking his head)* I think I'd rather forget that moment with him.

GLADYS Why?

PIET   It was as if we were embarrassed by each other.

GLADYS   You didn't tell me that either. I'd imagined a warm reunion of old friends.

PIET   No, it wasn't quite that. But maybe it's not surprising. We were caught on the wrong foot. I certainly was. I didn't even know he had been released from jail and suddenly there he was walking toward me on Main Street.

GLADYS   Go on.

PIET   I never thought I'd feel like that with him . . . you know, forcing myself to make polite conversation as if he was somebody whose name I had forgotten. I asked him about Mavis and the children and that's when he said: "We're leaving, Piet." When I finally understood what he meant, I didn't know what to say. I still don't. All I could think of was to ask him and the family to come around for a farewell meal. He said, "Yes." That's all.

GLADYS   So if you hadn't bumped into him, you might not have seen him again.

PIET   *(Hurriedly)*   No. He said he intended coming out to see us and say good-by before leaving.

GLADYS   He left it very late.

PIET   I'm sure he's been busy . . . packing up and . . . it's a big move.

GLADYS   So there goes Steven! You're not left with much now are you? . . . Me! . . . And I don't think I qualify as a comrade. I don't want to rub salt into your wounds, Peter, but I can't help being just a little cynical at this moment about the "struggle" all of you were so passionately committed to. I used to think there was something wrong with me when I heard everyone carrying on about "the cause," "freedom," "the people." You see, I never thought things were as bad as you made out. Some of the talk even made me a little nervous. Yes! You never realized that, did you? You were too busy believing that life had a purpose and I was too ashamed to say it made me nervous. But I can remember very clearly how frightened some of the talk made me. "Overthrowing the regime" sounded very violent to me. *(With a little laugh)* Not much chance of that now, is there, with everybody . . . how did you put it? . . . crawled away into his own little shell. Snails aren't the most revolutionary of God's creatures.

PIET They weren't empty slogans, Gladys. To misquote the Bard: The weakness lay not in our ideals, but in ourselves.

GLADYS Yes, of course. But not all of you surely? Just the one.

PIET What do you mean, my dear?

GLADYS Don't do that, Peter. You know very well what I mean. The informer. *(PIET doesn't respond)* I'm not imagining things, am I? Just before I went away wasn't everybody whispering about there being an informer in the group? And that is how the police . . .

PIET Yes, yes. You're right.

39

GLADYS *(Finishing the sentence with quiet deliberation)*
. . . and that is how the police knew that Steven was going to break his Banning Order and be at the party.

PIET I said you were right, my dear.

GLADYS Have you never worked out who it was?

PIET No.

GLADYS Did you try?

PIET Oh yes. I spent a lot of time doing that while you were away.

GLADYS And?

PIET I stopped myself.

GLADYS Why?

PIET I discovered that if I tried hard enough I could find a good reason for suspecting everyone. I wouldn't have had any friends left if I carried on.

GLADYS But on the face of it you haven't, Peter.

PIET Steve and five other friends are on their way to us at this very moment. Let me see if I can remember my toast. *(He studies his book of quotations)* "What is the odds so long as the fire of soul . . . is kindled at the taper of conviviality . . ."

GLADYS It's just as well, I suppose, that I decided not to go to that party. I would have been a very likely suspect.

PIET I don't think so, my dear.

GLADYS Not to you, obviously. But I'm sure the others would have had their doubts. After all, it was no secret that I didn't share everyone else's enthusiasm for "the cause." *(PIET remains absorbed in his book of quotations.)* It's no use, Peter.

PIET What?

GLADYS I'm sorry, but I've got to ask it. Do the others think it's you?

PIET *(Trying very hard to avoid her question)* I told you, my dear, on my side I could find a good reason . . .

GLADYS Peter. Do all the others think it's you?

PIET I don't know.

GLADYS Are you lying to me, or yourself?
(She waits)

PIET Yes. It looks as if . . . they all think . . . I'm the one.

GLADYS What about Steven?

PIET No! He wouldn't be coming here if he thought that.

GLADYS He's not here yet.

PIET He didn't cross to the other side of the street when he saw me coming.

GLADYS *(Outraged)* Who did that?

PIET It doesn't matter.

GLADYS *(Quietly)* My God! I want to scream. Maybe swearing would be better. How long have you known?

PIET It isn't something I "know" in that way. There's no one day on which a drought starts. But there were meetings to which I wasn't invited and then, as I said, I realized people were avoiding me. There is only one conclusion.

GLADYS And you didn't tell me because you thought it would aggravate my condition. Didn't you know I'd realize it sooner or later? I haven't been made that insensitive.

PIET It's not as simple as that, Gladys. Obviously I wanted to avoid upsetting you. But even without that, could we have talked about it? *(He speaks with deep emotion)* Sat down and discussed over supper the fact that I was considered a traitor? That's the correct word. Could you have made a simple entry to that effect in your diary? God! It's the ugliest thing that has ever happened to me. It makes me feel more ashamed of . . . myself, my fellow men . . . of everything! . . . in a way I never thought possible. *(*GLADYS *has been watching him very carefully)* What's the matter?

GLADYS I'm trying to see you as others do.

PIET And?

GLADYS It's not true, is it?
      *(*PIET *stares back at her for a long time before turning away)*

PIET   *(Vacantly . . . looking at his wrist watch)*   They should be here any minute now. I'll . . . I'll light the candles.

GLADYS   *(Getting up, she goes to the table)*   Yes, it looks very good. I'm going inside. Call me . . . if they come.
(She walks into the house, leaving PIET *alone in the backyard)*

Curtain

Act Two

The backyard about two hours later. PIET *is still waiting. He looks at his watch and after a moment's hesitation, he goes into the house and puts on the outside light. He returns to the backyard, blows out the candles and starts to clear the table.*

After a few seconds he hears the "Marseillaise" being played on a harmonica in the darkness beyond the backyard gate. PIET *hurriedly resets the table.* STEVE *appears out of the darkness.*

STEVE *(Respectfully, but with an exaggerated degree of authority)* Excuse me, sir! *(He flashes some sort of identity card)* Security Branch. I wonder if you could help me?

PIET *(Playing along)* Yes, my good man. What can I do for you?

STEVE I'm looking for a mad Afrikaner, who recites English poetry. He stays around here somewhere.

PIET *(Pretending outrage)* A what?

STEVE His name is Piet Bezuidenhout.

PIET Did I hear you right? An Afrikaner, reciting English poetry! And a Bezuidenhout at that!

STEVE I told you he was mad, sir.

47

PIET It's worse than that my good man. There's a name for his sort. Why do you think we lost the Boer War? And what do you think is making your people so cheeky these days?

STEVE *(Whips off his hat; is suddenly servile)* Sorry, sir.

PIET Subversive elements like him. English poetry! If I was you I would choose my company more carefully in future.

STEVE Is it all right if I visit you instead, then?

PIET Have you got a bottle? *(STEVE produces a bottle of wine from the side pocket of his jacket and holds it up)* Come inside.

STEVE Thank you, sir. *(He lets himself into the backyard)*

PIET *(Moving to the house)* They've arrived, Gladys!

STEVE *(Obviously very embarrassed)* Hold on, Piet! Hold on, man! I'm alone. Mavis couldn't make it. Charmaine has come down with something. Looks like the flu. With the trip coming up so soon, Mavis thought it best to stay at home with the children.

PIET Don't give it a thought. I'm sorry to hear about Charmaine, but if my memory doesn't fail me, the two of us were enough for a good time in the past.

STEVE *(With forced exuberance)* Right! Where do we start? *(Before PIET can answer)* Ja, of course! You ready? *(STEVE puts down his hat, buttons up his jacket, adopts a very formal stance and then launches into a recital of Longfellow's "The Slaves' Dream")*

Beside the ungathered rice he lay,
   His sickle in his hand;
His breast was bare, his matted hair
   Was buried in the sand.
Again, in the mist and shadow of sleep,
   He saw his Native Land.

Wide through the landscape of his dreams
   The lordly Niger flowed;
Beneath the palm-trees on the plain
   Once more a king he strode;
And heard the tinkling caravans
   Descend the mountain road.

He saw once more his dark-eyed queen
   Among her children stand;
They clasped his neck, they kissed his cheeks,
   They held him by the hand!—
A tear burst from the sleeper's lids
   And fell into the sand.

And then at furious speed he rode
   Along the Niger's bank;
His bridle-reins were golden chains,
   And, with a martial clank,
At each leap he could feel his scabbard of steel
   Smiting his stallion's flank.

Before him, like a blood-red flag,
   The bright flamingoes flew;
From morn till night he followed their flight,
   O'er plains where the tamarind grew,
Till he saw the roofs of Caffre huts,
   And the ocean rose to view.

At night he heard the lion roar,
　And the hyena scream,
And the river-horse, as he crushed the reeds
　Beside some hidden stream;
And it passed, like a glorious roll of drums,
　Through the triumph of his dream.

The forests, with their myriad tongues,
　Shouted of liberty;
And the Blast of the Desert cried aloud,
　With a voice so wild and free,
That he started in his sleep and smiled
　At their tempestuous glee.

He did not feel the driver's whip,
　Nor the burning heat of day;
For Death had illumined the Land of Sleep,
　And his lifeless body lay
A worn-out fetter, that the soul
　Had broken and thrown away!

(STEVE's *delivery is awkward and amateurish and*
before long he starts floundering for the words. PIET
prompts him to start with, but eventually takes over.
STEVE, *one beat behind, struggles to keep up as* PIET
gets into his stride and then gallops splendidly to the
end of the poem. We are obviously watching a little
scene that has taken place many times in the past. The
effect is both comic and moving. When it is finished,
there is a pause as the two men look at each other)

PIET　*(Quietly)*　Welcome, Steve.

STEVE　Hello, you mad Afrikaner.

PIET *(Embarrassed by the emotion he feels)* I'll get the wine.

STEVE *(Handing over his bottle)* Let's open mine!

PIET This puts my humble offering to shame. We'll save it for the feast. Have you eaten?

STEVE Later.

PIET Make yourself at home, man! Take off your coat. The night is still young.

STEVE Okay. Bring on the dancing girls!
(PIET goes into the house . . . the bedroom. GLADYS is sitting at her dressing table)

PIET Steve's arrived.

GLADYS I heard his voice. And the others?

PIET No. Charmaine is sick. That's why he's late. Mavis stayed behind to look after her. Come and join us, my dear, even if it's only for a few minutes. Let's end the day on a happy note. It's the Steve we knew. He wouldn't have come if everything wasn't all right.

GLADYS I will. Just leave me for a little while.
(PIET rejoins STEVE in the backyard)

PIET *(Holding up a bottle of wine)* "A draught of vintage that hath been cooled a long age in the deep delved refrigerator!" I told you to take off your coat, man! You look like a bloody bank manager. *(His happiness knows no bounds)* Hell, Steve, this calls for a toast.

STEVE Just as long as I don't have to make a speech.

PIET *(Laughing at a memory)* I can remember an occasion when that did not present a problem.

STEVE When was that?

PIET Your very first visit to us here. No? *(He raises his glass)* "To the birth of a man!" Come on, Steve! What's the matter with you? My godson.

STEVE Hey, by the way! Little Pietertjie's birth.

PIET That's right. We were still busy unpacking and sorting things out in there when you arrived from the hospital.

STEVE Of course. Hell, Piet, that goes back a few years now, hey? He turns seven next birthday. I couldn't believe it when they woke me up in the waiting room and said: "It's a boy, at last, Mr. Daniels." What the hell was it you wanted me to call him again?

PIET Gorki . . . and I still think you should have done it.

STEVE Haaikona Piet! *You* go to school with a name like that and see what the other kids do to you.

PIET To hell with them! Gorki Daniels! It's got a ring to it, man.

STEVE That was quite a night, hey?

PIET Memorable, my friend. Memorable. Obviously, there had to be a toast to your son, and a speech from you.

STEVE Then one to the house, and a speech from you!

PIET What came next? The future!

STEVE That was a speech from both of us, wasn't it?

PIET Correct. I proposed, you replied. But the trouble really started when we decided that a general toast to the comrades was not good enough, that all of them merited individual recognition. And if you remember, our membership was quite healthy in those days.

STEVE Ja, no chance of getting drunk on that now, hey? So there's our toast. To the good old days! If nothing else, they produced a few revolutionary hangovers.

PIET *(Restraining him from emptying his glass, and raising his own)* "What is the odds . . ."*(PIET has forgotten the toast. His spectacles and little book of quotations come out hurriedly)* "What is the odds so long . . ."*(He finds the correct page)* "What is the odds so long as the fire of soul is kindled at the taper of conviviality and the wing of friendship never moults a feather."

STEVE Jesus, Bezuidenhout! How the hell do you do it?

PIET What?

STEVE All your quotations and poetry. You should have been a schoolteacher, man.

PIET I tried to be a farmer, Steve, and the poetry starts where that ends . . . with a few seconds of silence out in the veld under a very hot sun.

53

STEVE You've never told me that one.

PIET I know, but only because I've tried very hard to forget it. And I thought I had . . . but it's been a lot in my thoughts lately.

STEVE What happened?

PIET Nothing. That's the whole point to the story . . . nothing. One of the last little chores of Baas Bezuidenhout on the farm was to put on his black suit and join an African family that had worked for him—and his father before him—around a little grave out in the veld. A baby had died. Gastroenteritis. There hadn't been a drop of clean water on Alwynlaagte . . . the farm . . . for God alone knows how many months. They hadn't "dug" that hole, Steve. They'd used a pick and crowbars to break into the ground, it was so dry. Anyway . . . when it came to my turn to say a few words . . . (PIET *shakes his head*) That hole with the little homemade coffin at the bottom defeated me. I had dug plenty of them as deep as that, but to plant trees or fence posts, or to lay in a dipping tank. A sense of deep, personal failure overwhelmed me. They waited—I don't know how long—until I just shook my head and walked away. I lasted out another three months on the farm, and that is how I passed the time. There was this little book of poetry and stories in the house. I read through it many times, looking for something I could have said out there in the veld.

STEVE Did Baas Bezuidenhout ever find it?

PIET No. But I learned a few poems while trying. Seen any of the old crowd since you've been out?

STEVE   Only Solly. He's been damned good, helping us with our boat tickets, you know, and everything. Got his lawyer to sort out the Exit Permit and to have my Banning Order relaxed for these last few weeks. But he's the only one.

PIET   Yes, things have been very quiet lately.

STEVE   So he was saying. But even if they weren't, I don't want to know or talk about it.

PIET   I was just wondering . . .

STEVE   No, sure, sure. It's just that I've had enough, Piet.

PIET   I understand.
(An awkward silence between the two men is broken by GLADYS*'s appearance)*

GLADYS   Hello, Steven!

STEVE   Gladys! Long time no see, hey!
(They shake hands. STEVE *and* GLADYS *treat each other with a stilted politeness and formality)*

PIET   Good to see him here again, isn't it?

GLADYS   Yes, it is. I'm sorry Mavis couldn't come. Peter told me about . . . which one is it that's sick?

STEVE   Charmaine.

GLADYS   What a lovely name.

STEVE   Mavis is also sorry she couldn't make it. She really was looking forward to seeing you again.

PIET   *(Pulling out her chair)*   Here, my dear. A glass of sherry?

55

GLADYS Yes, please. *(*PIET *walks into the house)*

GLADYS And bring out the plate of snacks! I put them in the fridge. *(Turning to* STEVE*)* We'd given up hope of seeing you.

STEVE Ja, sorry about everything. *(Trying to break the ice)* So, how things been with you, Gladys?

GLADYS Oh, just the same old humdrum existence. I putter about the house and Peter goes for long walks in the veld looking for aloes.

STEVE Ja, so I see. *(Gesturing at the aloes)* This is all new.

GLADYS Peter's new hobby, now that there's no politics left. Aloes. He takes it very seriously. He's got a little book and he knows all their names.

STEVE I prefer flowers myself.

GLADYS That makes two of us. We tried to lay out a little flower bed here once . . . Roses! . . . But the soil is very poor. Come, let's sit down. So, Steven, you're on your way to England. I couldn't believe my ears when Peter told me.

STEVE Next week.

GLADYS So I gather. You're very fortunate, you know.

STEVE You reckon so, Gladys?

GLADYS To be leaving this country! You don't have any doubts, surely? You of all people.

STEVE *(With an embarrassed little laugh)* Well, the children are excited, that I can say for sure.

GLADYS And so they should be. It will be a marvelous experience. Travel broadens the mind.

STEVE Ja, I'm glad for their sakes. It's just that I don't know how much broadening mine can take. I'm forty-two, Gladys, and I've spent most of those years here in Port Elizabeth. It's going to be a big change.

GLADYS But for the better. You must think positively.

STEVE You're right. It's hard to imagine anything worse than the past years. *(Trying to move the conversation along)* One thing I can say is that I'm not looking forward to the boat trip too much.

GLADYS One of the mail ships?

STEVE *Windsor Castle.* I know I'm going to be seasick all the way! And I can't swim, you know.

GLADYS You're joking.

STEVE Truly. I love my fishing, but when it comes to getting into that water . . . ! No, thank you!

GLADYS Well, don't worry about it. They've got lifebelts and all sorts of things that will keep you floating in case something happens . . . which is most unlikely.

STEVE What's it going to be like, Gladys?

GLADYS What?

STEVE England. All I know about it is what I've seen on the bioscope and pictures in books. They always make it look very pretty. *(She is staring at him)* Is it really like that?

GLADYS Why do you ask me?

STEVE You're from England, aren't you?

GLADYS What makes you say that?

STEVE Oh, your manners and the way you speak. Not rough and ready like Piet and myself. Sorry . . . I always thought . . .

GLADYS That's all right. In a way I suppose I am from England . . . now. *(She gives a little smile)* I've been there many times.

STEVE Tell me about it.

GLADYS What do you want to know, Steven?

STEVE Anything. Very cold in winter, hey? Solly warned me about that. He's been over a couple of times. That's all little Beryl talks about . . . making a snowman. Did you ever do that?

GLADYS No. There are no snowmen in my memories.

STEVE But it's summer there now.

GLADYS *(Another smile)* Of course. It will never be anything else. *(Before she can say anything more the backyard light goes out)* Oh dear! What's happened now?

STEVE The light's gone, Piet!

PIET   *(Calls from offstage)*   Oh no, it hasn't. *(PIET comes out of the house carrying the two brass candlesticks—the candles alight—a plate of snacks and a glass of sherry)* "Put out the light, and then put out the light./If I quench thee thou flaming minister/I can thy former light store should I repent me./But once put out thy light . . ."

STEVE   Fancy stuff, hey!

PIET   How's your glass?

STEVE   *(Emptying it)*   Empty.

PIET   And now, ladies and gentlemen, to keep the tradition alive, another toast. To your new pastures! *(They all raise their glasses)*

GLADYS   New pastures.

STEVE   Ja, Gladys was telling me about them.

GLADYS   Later.

PIET   All packed and ready for the big move?

STEVE   Ag no man, Piet!

PIET   What's the matter?

STEVE   You promised me a good time.

PIET   And you're going to get it.

STEVE   Then don't ask questions like that. Packed up and ready? You must be joking. If you really want to know what that is all about, Piet, you just go sit in your lounge with some empty suitcases and boxes and let Gladys start to empty the drawers and the cupboards and the wardrobe and pile it all around you. And then you must choose, hey! What you want to take with you, what you'll give to your old Auntie Bettie in Salisbury Park or what you'll just maar throw away. *(Shaking his head ruefully)* I don't know where we kept it all, Gladys. Mavis just keeps coming with more and more . . . and then the children! Please pack this, Daddy, please pack that, Daddy. You ought to see the place. It looks as if burglars have been in the house ransacking it. And you know me, Piet! I'm one for having things nice and tidy. I've packed and unpacked those bloody suitcases I don't know how many times already, trying to fit in all the damned things. Excuse the language, Gladys, but that is how I feel about it. When I left the house to come here tonight I put my foot in my own face—our wedding photo! . . . so that started Mavis crying . . . you know, bad luck!—and then I stood on that table lamp covered with seashells. You know the one, Piet, with all the mother-of-pearl. My dad made it. It was going to be my special souvenir of this place in our home over there.

GLADYS   I'm sure you'll be able to fix it, Steven.

STEVE   Maybe. I didn't even look to see how broken it was, I was so the hell-in, Gladys. Just slammed the door on the lot . . . wife, children, suitcases, broken glass . . . (PIET *laughs*)   It's no joke, man. It's a life lying around on that lounge floor like a pile of rubbish. That's what I'm trying to squeeze into a few old suitcases. And the worst part is that you start to hate it. Sometimes I think we should just chuck the whole lot away. Get onto that boat with a pair of pajamas each and a toothbrush. Start over there with nothing. But there's no winning. Because just when you're feeling like that, out of a box or a cupboard drawer comes something you'd forgotten about . . . and before you know it, you're sitting there on the floor smiling at a memory. *(He goes through his coat pockets and finds an old snapshot)* Get your glasses.

PIET *(He puts on his spectacles and takes the snapshot)* What do I see?

STEVE Me and my dad.

PIET And this?

STEVE Hell, you are blind. Can't you see? It's a fish. Look again.

PIET Hell, Steve, it's big!

STEVE *(Proudly)* Of course, that's just it. Why do you think we found somebody with a camera and a spool? And in Fairview. *(Studies it himself)* How can I throw this away? Want to see, Gladys? Me and my dad.

GLADYS You look just like him.

STEVE It was the biggest moment in the old man's life. And I was there when he caught it. Maitland surf! Friday afternoons after work we used to trek out from Fairview on his bike. Winter, it was dark before we were halfway there. Hell, that last stretch across the sand was a slog! He made me push the bike, and I was still only a pikkie. We had one hole we always fished. And he caught, hey! The white boys used to come past with their fancy rods and reels empty-handed, while we had Steenbras tails flapping around us on the sand. The old man had patience. That was his secret. I can still see him . . . sitting next to the fire, his rod in front of him . . . waiting, for the big one. *(He laughs)* And that night it came. Piet . . . ! With its first run it walked him down the beach and into the darkness. He managed to turn its head and get it back to our spot, and then it was off again. Three times! With me next to him shouting: "Don't lose it, Daddy! Don't lose it!" The reel seized up. Solid! But by then the fish had had it as well. He pulled it in hand over hand. A thirty pound bloody musselcracker! It lay there on the sand like a sack of potatoes while we cried with happiness. But the real fun came the next morning trying to get it onto the bicycle. He wouldn't gut and scale it. Not a damn! Fairview had to see it the way it was when he caught it. We ended up tying it to the crossbar and walking home, him pushing and me behind holding up the tail. Haai! That old man!

PIET *(Filling glasses)* What was his full name?

STEVE Willem Gerhardus Daniels. But everybody just called him Uncle Willie.

PIET I like the Willem Gerhardus. That name belongs to this world as surely as any one of those aloes. I'd like to raise my glass to Willem Gerhardus Daniels.

(GLADYS *does the same. There is a pause . . .* STEVE *shakes his head)*

STEVE   No, don't let's get sentimental about him, Piet.

PIET   I meant it, Steve.

STEVE   I'm sure you did. It's just that if you'd seen him at the end you wouldn't want to do that. All he wanted from life was to work, feed his family and wait for another big one. That's not asking for a lot, hey? But it was still too much for a Coloured man. They kicked us out, Gladys. Separate Group Areas. Fairview was declared white and that was the end of us. Every penny he had saved was taken by the lawyers. He tried to fight it, you see. Petitions and court cases that went on and on. When we finally piled our furniture onto the back of the lorry he was broke. That was quite a day! The old man took out his Bible and cursed that little bit of ground before we drove away. It's still standing empty, you know. No whitey has built on it yet. Strange the things you remember! We had an auntie staying with us. She was a bit simple. I worked it out the other day . . . my father's brother-in-law's sister-in-law . . . Ja! Anyway, it was she and me on the back of the lorry on top of the furniture, me with the chickens and the old auntie with a big pumpkin in her lap! But that finished Willem Gerhardus. He hadn't just lost his house and his savings, they also took away the sea. I mean . . . how the hell do you get from Salt Lake to Maitland on a bicycle?! He tried the river a few times, but that wasn't for him. I'll never forget one day in the backyard there at Salt Lake. I had

63

started to get a bit conscious about things, and I was going on about our rights and what have you. He just listened. When I was finished he shook his head and said: "Ons geslag is verkeerd." Hell, that made me angry! And I told him we have only ourselves to blame if we let them walk over us. He just shook his head and repeated himself: "Ons geslag is verkeerd." Sorry, Gladys. That means . . . how would you say it nice in English, Piet?

PIET Our generation . . . our race is a mistake.

STEVE Ja, something like that. And maybe he was right after all. *(He pauses)* I like the sound of my own voice tonight, hey, Gladys?

GLADYS Don't apologize for that. So do I! I'm just sorry your memories are so-so.

STEVE You're very polite. I hope they're all like you in England.

GLADYS I'm not being polite, Steven. I meant it. We haven't had a visitor for a long time. Isn't that so, Peter?

PIET Yes, that's true.

GLADYS And with Steven leaving, heaven alone knows when we'll get another. That's a disturbing thought, isn't it? You could find yourself talking to your aloes for quite a long time yet, you know.

PIET *(He is uneasy about the direction the conversation is taking. He turns to his aloes)* What do you think of them, Steve? So far I've got nine of the indigenous

64

Eastern Cape species. There's twenty all told. Not bad for six months, is it?

GLADYS *(To* STEVE) You see, there is no chance of persuading him to leave. I must confess I don't really understand why. It's all got to do with him being an Afrikaner and this being "home" . . . because like you, Steven, I'm more than prepared to call some other place that. But not Peter. If those aloes can survive droughts, so can he!

PIET Come. Let me show you the collection. *(He puts on the outside light)* Right. Where do we begin? These two. Both saponarias. You wouldn't think so, would you? The range of variation within a species is quite remarkable. "Nature refusing to be shackled by the fetters of a man-made system." Here we have ferox . . . arborescens . . . ciliaris . . . it's a sort of climbing aloe. Pushes its way through dense undergrowth to reach the sun. *(To* GLADYS) All right, my dear? *(Back to* STEVE) What I would really like to do, Steve, is get in a few nice rocks and a load of good red soil and build a little natural habitat in this corner . . . for the dwarf species.

STEVE You were surprised when I told you I was pulling out, weren't you?

GLADYS Surprised? That's putting it mildly, Steven. It left him speechless. He only managed to tell me tonight. It might not have been so bad if it was one of the others . . . but you, of all people!

PIET *(Quietly to* GLADYS) Let me speak for myself.

GLADYS   Haven't I told the truth?

PIET   *(Turning to* STEVE*)*   Yes, I was . . . but is that so strange, Steve?

STEVE   No, of course not. I was just saying . . . But then, what did you expect, Piet? That I would come out of jail, go home quietly and sit out the rest of my Banning Order? And when that was up and they slap on another five years, just go on sitting there waiting for charity from the comrades to feed my family? That's a hell of a contribution to the struggle! Or does the cause need a few martyrs now to get it going again? I'm not going to be one, Piet.

PIET   You're also doing it, Steve. Don't put words in my mouth. I think I understand.

STEVE   What?

PIET   Your reasons for leaving.

STEVE   What are they?

PIET   Hell, Steve . . . !

STEVE   I'm being serious, man! I want to know how much you understand.

PIET   Let's talk about something else, Steve.

STEVE   Ag, come on, Piet! There's no time left for polite conversation. And certainly not between the two of us. Here, look at that. *(He produces a card from his back pocket and throws it down on the table)* My membership card of the Amalgamated Building Workers Union of South Africa. It certifies that

Steven Daniels is a qualified bricklayer and mason. Four years apprenticeship and twenty years experience. You know what that means, Piet? *(Holding out his hands)* These are useful. They can do a job, and they can do it bloody well. The G.M. plant at the bottom of Kempston Road . . . I laid two thousand four hundred bricks there one day, Piet. Using these is the only way I can feed and clothe my family. I've got nothing else! They haven't worked for four years now. Look at them. They're softer than Mavis's. They might as well fall off for all they mean in my life now. And I must feel guilty about leaving?

PIET Steve . . .

STEVE No, let me finish. I've paid my debts in full, Piet. I don't owe this damned country a thing anymore. And let me tell you something, if they ever get their hands on you, you'll feel the same. You'll also get out.

PIET You're arguing with yourself, Steve. I haven't accused you of anything.

STEVE Thanks, Piet. That's big of you. But if ever you want to, just remember it's easier for you.

PIET I know that.

STEVE If I had a white skin, I'd also find lots of reasons for not leaving this country. *(He pauses, then sits down in a chair)* Hell, that's crude! Doesn't sound like the Steve Daniels you used to know, hey? Sorry people . . . sorry, sorry. Jesus, I spend a lot of time

67

apologizing for myself nowadays. If it's any excuse,
I'm just as bad at home. Mavis says I left my manners behind in jail.

GLADYS Oh dear, is the party over?
  *(Neither man responds. She gets up and quietly starts
  to stack plates and cutlery)*

PIET *(The unidentified aloe in his hands)* I found this
one this morning, but I'm buggered if I can iden-
tify it.

STEVE I've lost more than just my manners, Piet.
There was nothing to do inside, when they weren't
questioning me, except think. So I did a lot of that.
Too much, I suppose, but what the hell! You can't
stop yourself. It all came down to one question, Piet.
Why was I really there, inside? Don't tell me about
the party at Betty's and the Special Branch catching
me having a drink, singing freedom songs on the
sly, with the comrades. That's not what I mean. My
life had been in a mess long before they walked in
that night. Why? And for what? You understand
what I'm asking? Tell me one thing we've achieved
that makes it worthwhile staying here and messing
up my children's lives the way I have mine. Because
that's what will happen. We've only seen it get
worse. And it's going to go on getting worse. But I
know why now. We were like a bunch of boy scouts
playing at politics. Those boer-boys play the game
rough. It's going to need men who don't care about
the rules to sort them out. That was never us.

GLADYS I'll leave the wine.

STEVE My turn for a toast! Your glass all right, Gladys? *(He fills up his own)* I always had a feeling you never cared much for our politics. Here's your chance. *(He raises his glass)* What do they call it, Piet? A lost cause!
  (GLADYS exits into the house with the dinnerware)

PIET My turn to say no. I won't raise my glass to that.

STEVE *(Studying him carefully before speaking)* You confuse the issue for me. I got no problems with old Solly in his nice house out at Humewood. He gives me boat tickets, I give him an easy conscience. And anyway, he's got a factory full of my people making him richer. I'm not saying his heart isn't in the right place. Hell man, he's proved it! Same for the others. They all got their hearts in the right place . . . *(A sudden bitterness comes into his voice)* . . . so I got no problems in saying good-by to them next week. Because I know I'll see them all over there if it ever gets rough for them as well! *(GLADYS returns)* But you? No, Gladys is right. I can't see you doing that. Piet Bezuidenhout will be here at the end even if it means being the last one left. You're fooling yourself, Piet, if you think there's any hope. Do what I'm doing, man. Get out. Join me in England. We can sit back and talk as much and as loud as we like . . . because that's all we ever did here. Somebody was telling me there's a place over there where you can stand up on a box and say anything you like.

GLADYS Poor Peter! It's all gone wrong, hasn't it? *(To STEVE)* He had such high hopes for this reunion with you. I wasn't exaggerating when I said he talks

69

to his aloes. That's all he's got left for company. You see, the others have been avoiding us as if we had the plague. At first I thought it was because of me . . . I haven't been too well lately . . . but we know the real reason now, not that it helps very much. They all suspect Peter of being a police informer. Did you know that? Yes. They all think he is the one who told them you were going to be at that party. *(GLADYS goes into the house with another load from the table. The two men stare at each other. GLADYS returns)* What about you, Steven?

PIET   No, Gladys! Enough's been said.

GLADYS   *(Ignoring PIET)* I think he does as well, Peter. Or at least has doubts. That's why Mavis didn't come, isn't it? Have I embarrassed you, Steven? There's no need to be. We're all old friends, and anyway, it's better to have these things out in the open. I'm sure you've been thinking about it. Watching him all night and trying to decide.

PIET   Please, Gladys!

GLADYS   *(Violently)* No. No! Haven't you had enough lies! Who are they meant to protect this time? Him? Your beautiful friendship? Can't you see it's rotten with doubt? Don't leave us in suspense, Steven. What have you decided? Take a good look at him. Nothing? Still just doubts? Then let me settle them for you. *(She pauses, then turns and stares at PIET)* It happens to be the truth. Yes. He is an informer. Peter is the one who went to the police and told them you were going to break your Banning Order and be at the party.

PIET *(Staring at her in disbelief)* No . . .

GLADYS Yes! I'll swear to it on your Bible if you want me to!

PIET Gladys . . .

GLADYS Don't touch me!

STEVE Hell! Wine has gone to my head. This is quite a party. Ja, you guessed right, Gladys. That's why Mavis isn't here. There's nothing wrong with the children. It's just that she's got *no* doubts. She is certain it was you, Piet. I had a hell of an argument with her before coming here. She said it was a trap. I told her and the kids to go to hell . . . nearly tore up the boat tickets. That's why I was late . . . plus the fact that I had a few drinks on the way. I needed Dutch courage to face you. *(He pauses)* Piet?

PIET Nothing to say.

STEVE *(Disbelief shows on his face)* Nothing . . . ? You're joking, Piet.

PIET I got nothing to say, Steve.
     (A few seconds of silence and then STEVE *starts laughing)*

STEVE Jesus, that's funny! I'm sorry, Piet, but I mean it. That's very, very funny. I think those were my exact words when they started questioning me after the party. They made a few jokes in the car, but I kept quiet . . . you see, hiding there in Betty's wardrobe while they searched the place . . . squashed in the dark there among her clothes . . . with her perfume and me shit-scared . . . it came up, man. Hard!

I was trying to hit the damned thing down when they found me. And they saw it. In the car one of them said: "If you don't teach it to behave, Daniels, we'll take it away from you." I was scared, Piet. I knew where I was going. Anyway, up there on the fifth floor the questions really started. And Steve Daniels replied: "I've got nothing to say." *(He laughs again)* You want to know how they made me change my mind? There's a room up there on the fifth floor . . . they call it the waiting room. All it's got is a chair by an open window. Every time I said that . . . "Nothing to say!" . . . and I kept it up for a long time, Piet! . . . they put me in there and left me alone. Every half hour or so a couple of them would stick their heads in, look at me . . . and laugh. I got no bruises to show you. That's all they ever did to me. Just laugh. But they kept it up. One night back in my cell, after another day of that, I knew that if they put me in there once more . . . I'd jump. And I wasn't thinking of escape from five floors up. Ja! They had laughed at my manhood and every reason I had for diving out of that window. When they came to fetch me the next morning I was crying like a baby. And they comforted me like I was one. When they started their questions again, I wiped my eyes and answered . . . for the first time. I told them everything. Every bloody thing I knew. And if they'd wanted it, I would have told them things I didn't know. But wait . . . the really *big* laugh is still coming. When I had finished and signed my statement, they patted me on the back and said: "Well done, Daniels! But now tell us something we don't know." And they weren't fooling. They knew everything. Somebody had been talking to them for a long time, and about a hell of a lot more than Steve Daniels sneaking out to have a good time. So for Christ's sake, Piet, anything you like . . . a lie if it's necessary . . . but don't tell me you got nothing to say!

PIET   A lie?

STEVE   All right! I'll admit it. I've got doubts. So I'm asking you straight: Is Gladys telling the truth?

PIET   Why me, Steve?

GLADYS   Careful, Steven! He looks like one of them, doesn't he? The same gross certainty in himself! He certainly sounds like them. He speaks English with a dreadful accent. What else, Steven? He's poor enough to do it for money.

STEVE   All right Gladys! *(He grabs his jacket, hesitates for a second, then goes over to confront* PIET *directly)* Relax, Piet. I've solved our problem. I'm going to hope it was you. I mean it. I'm going to try hard, because, hell, man! . . . will that make it easier going next week . . . if I can throw away our friendship like all that junk on my lounge floor.
    (He turns to go)

GLADYS   *(To* PIET*)*   You're not going to defend yourself and deny it?

PIET   No.

GLADYS   My God, are you that safe? Can nothing threaten you? I'm so jealous, Peter. Aren't you, Steven?

STEVE   Gladys?

GLADYS   Wouldn't you like to be as safe as he is? Because we aren't, you know.

STEVE   Please, Gladys! What's going on? Are you playing games?

GLADYS   You wouldn't be doubting him if you were. I doubt everything now. But not him. When you come to think of it, it's almost stupid. He's lost a farm, his friends . . . you! . . . the great purpose in his life, and he's going to lose a lot more before it's all over, but his faith in himself refuses to be shaken. Of course he didn't do it! What's happened to you, Steven? He isn't an informer. It must have been one of your other trusted comrades. Go back to Mavis and start all over again, because it wasn't him.

STEVE   *(Angrily)*   Then why did you . . . ?

GLADYS   *(Violently)*   That's my business. Yes, mine! My reason for telling you an ugly lie, which you were ready to believe! . . . is *my* business. I accept, Steven, that I am just a white face on the outskirts of your terrible life, but I'm in the middle of mine and yours is just a brown face on the outskirts of that. Do you understand what I'm saying? I've got my own story. I don't need yours. I've discovered hell for myself. It might be hard for you to accept, Steven, but you are not the only one who has been hurt. Politics and black skins don't make the only victims in this country.

STEVE   Gladys . . .

74

PIET   Leave her alone, Steve.

GLADYS   *(Turning on him with equal violence)*   I don't
need you! I don't need you to protect me anymore!
You never did, anyway. When they took away my
diaries you did nothing. When the others took away
my false teeth and held me down and blew my mind
to pieces, you weren't even there! I called for you,
Peter, but you weren't there.

PIET   *(Restraining* GLADYS *physically)*   I think you'd
better go, Steve!

GLADYS   No, he can't! *(She stops struggling and speaks
pleadingly)*   Please . . . please . . . I promised to tell
him about England. I was taught to keep my prom-
ises. *(*PIET *releases her. She steadies herself and speaks
calmly)*   It's very green. There are mountains in the
distance, but you can't see them too clearly because
of a soft, soft mist and the rays of the setting sun.
There's a lovely little cottage with a thatch roof, and
flowers in the garden, and winding past it an old
country road with tall trees along the side. An old
shepherd and his dog are herding a little flock of
sheep along it and watching them, at the garden
gate, is a little girl . . . It's called "Sunset in Somer-
set" and it hangs on a wall in a room where you sit
and wait for your turn. I always tried to forget what
was coming by looking at it and imagining that I
was the little girl and that I lived in that cottage. But
it didn't really help because the door to the room
where they do it goes on opening and closing, opening and closing and you get nearer and nearer
. . . I had a friend. Marlene. She'd been there for

a long time already. We used to sit together. She saw I was frightened. "Do you know any swear words?" she asked me. "It will make you feel better. Go on, swear, man. As hard as you can." She taught me. Oh shit! Oh fucking, almighty, bloody, Jesus Christ . . . ! But even that didn't help, because when your turn does come and they call your name and you sit down on the floor and say "No," they pick you up and carry you inside . . . and do it. They've burned my brain as brown as yours, Steven. *(Her little present for Mavis is in front of her on the table. She examines it vacantly for a few seconds, and then remembers. She gets up and goes over to* STEVE. *She speaks quietly and calmly)* A little something for Mavis. Tell her I wish her bon voyage. Good-by, Steve.

> *(She goes into the house. The two men avoid each other's eyes)*

STEVE *(Putting on his coat)* What happened?

PIET Those raids, after your arrest. They took away personal diaries she had been keeping. Then she started to get funny . . . imagining things. Wouldn't go out because people were spying on her. She thought I was one of the Special Branch.

STEVE Those bastards!

PIET That's why I couldn't get to your trial. The doctors told me not to leave her alone. Anyway, it got worse, and they took her away to Fort England Clinic.

STEVE *(He makes a half-hearted move to leave)* I don't want to leave this country, Piet. I was born here. It's my home. But they won't give me a chance to live. And they'll do the same to my children. You were prepared to let me go believing that you . . .

PIET   Hell, Steve, you know why. If you could have believed it, there was no point in denying it.

STEVE   Ja. So that's it, then. No quotation for old time's sake?

PIET   No. I'd rather remember this as another occasion when I didn't know what to say.
        (STEVE *puts on his hat and goes.* PIET *goes into the house and joins* GLADYS *in the bedroom. She is sitting at her dressing table with her diary*)

GLADYS   Has he gone?

PIET   Yes.

GLADYS   Did he say anything more?

PIET   No. Just good-by. There wasn't anything left to say.

GLADYS   I wrecked everything, didn't I?

PIET   Between Steve and me? No.

GLADYS   I tried.

PIET   There was nothing left to wreck.

GLADYS   (*Holding her diary*)   I should have wrapped this up as well and given it to him as his farewell present. It would have been appropriate. He's got to start his life again. I know what that means. In some ways that's the worst . . . starting again . . . waking up with nothing left, not even your name, and having to start again. You see, I wasn't able to use it. It's empty. Blank. *(Turning the pages)*   All of them . . . blank . . . blank. It wasn't for want of trying, Peter. I sat down every night, opened it . . . but then nothing. The ink used to clot and dry on the nib while I sat looking at the blank page. I've got no secrets left, except for one which I don't want. I've tried to find others in my life, but all I've got is this one, and I'm frightened of it. There's a little ritual at the end of every meal in Fort England. You sit at your table and wait while the dirty cutlery is taken to the matron, so that she can count the knives. There are none missing tonight, but . . . You're a good man, Peter, and that has become a terrible provocation. I want to destroy that goodness. Ironic, isn't it! That which I most hate and fear about this country is all I seem to have learned. *(She looks at her diary)*   I'll keep this and try next time. I've got to go back, Peter.

PIET   Are you sure?

GLADYS   Yes. Aren't you?
(She opens a drawer and starts to take out bottles of pills and toilet articles)

PIET   If you take some pills now, do you think we'll be all right until the morning?

GLADYS   Yes. Will you stay awake?

PIET   Yes.

GLADYS   And pack a suitcase for me?

PIET Yes.

GLADYS I'll go quietly this time.

PIET Do you want to go to bed now? *(She nods)*
Just call me if you want anything.
*(He leaves the bedroom. Gladys sits at her dressing
table quietly sorting out bottles of pills and a few
personal possessions, which she will take with her.
Piet, in the backyard, sits with the unidentified aloe)*

Curtain